It's Time To Get That Book Out Of You!

The Birth of an Author

Shall Be Born

The Power of the Author inside you deserves to live. "Discover" the author in you.

Parice C. Parker

It's Time To Get That Book Out Of You!

The Birth of an Author
Shall Be BORN

Copyright by:

Library of Congress 2013

ISBN: 978 -0-9910627-1- 3

Cover Design: Parice Parker

Author: Parice Parker

Editor: Phyllis R Brown

Fountain of Life Publisher's House

Printed in the United States of America

Parice C. Parker

It's Time To Get That Book Out Of You!

The Birth of an Author
Shall Be BORN

Fountain of Life Publishers House

P. O. Box 922612, Norcross, GA 30010
Phone: 404.936.3989
Please Send Manuscripts to Email:
publish@pariceparker.biz

For book orders or wholesale distribution
Website: www.pariceparker.biz

It's Time To Get That Book Out Of You!

The Birth of an Author Shall Be BORN

Table of Contents

Introduction

Parice C. Parker

It's Time To Get That Book Out Of You!

The Birth of an Author Shall Be BORN

What Inspired The Author To Write This Book?

I realized I had the gift to crank up the zeal of a writer. As I traveled, teaching creative writing, many contacted me wondering when I was coming to their area. I couldn't be all places at once. I was then motivated to allow my voice to speak to the writer's heart and tell them secrets of how to have a more successful writing journey. There are great techniques on completing a book from the introduction to the end. An unfinished and unpublished book is dead. That book inside deserves to live. A lot of people wanted me to mentor them through their book writing journey because they have witnessed how I have mastered book writing. The Birth of an Author Shall Be

It's Time To Get That Book Out Of You!

Born is purposed to get that book out of you. Push to give your new book an opportunity to live. Someone needs your book more than you need to write it. The Birth of an Author Shall Be Born, is it you? It's time to discover the author in you.

Parice Parker

It's Time To Get That Book Out Of You!

The Birth of an Author Shall Be BORN

Introduction

The birth of an author shall be born because we are creators. One thing I love about authors is that they have the power to form their own world to come. A mind is extremely creative and an author's concept of art has no limits. We are visionaries and see things others cannot. The power of an author is POTENT because they shape and mold through creation of thought. Our focus can be distracted but what's in our view we bring by inventing what we see. Regardless of our circumstances, an author will let their mind take them to a whole new world and that is where the shaping begins. As we draft on paper our hearts are led by the ink of a pen and the stroke of a key. We see doors that are shut fly wide open! We dream and then bring it to pass. An author will ride out their nightmares to see the fullness of their writing journey exist. The purpose of an author is to simply make what they see appear. Through the vision of an author we have the

It's Time To Get That Book Out Of You!

ability to dress our lives in expressive words just for others to visualize what we see. It is the desire in the heart that thrust the author to their destiny. Once the flame of writing grows intense in the heart of the writer its journey is complete. Authors do not compromise; they cause their dreams to come to life. Things you must know about writing a book and tips to help complete your writing journey are here. The birth of an author shall be born, is it you?

Parice C. Parker

It's Time To Get That Book Out Of You!

The Birth of an Author
Shall Be BORN

Authors are visionaries that publish to the world, what they see.

~ *Parice C. Parker*

It's Time To Get That Book Out Of You!

The Birth of an Author
Shall Be BORN

Chapter ONE
An Author in the Making

Yes, years ago I was telling everyone "I'm writing a book," and did not even have the first chapter complete. However, one day I grew to a point of NO RETURN. I completed my first book. When I received that book order, I immediately opened the

It's Time To Get That Book Out Of You!

box then cried because I finally saw my DREAM COME TO LIFE! I want the same for you because that story inside needs to come out. Imagine the potential once your book is complete. Imagine if I would not have written this book then you would not be reading it. To give your book life is the purpose of *The Birth of An Author Shall Be Born!*

Writing a book can be very complicated but with the right motives IT SHALL BE DONE! Do not go through another year telling everyone I am writing a book, and then never complete it. Once you read this book you will be EMPOWERED to FINISH. There are many things you as a writer need to know such as:

- *Overcoming Writers Block*

- *Placing Chapters*

- *Where Do I Start*

- *Strategies On Book Writing*

- *Getting To Know Your Book*

It's Time To Get That Book Out Of You!

- *Your Book Style*

- *Book Editing*

- *Marketing Your Book*

- *Discovering Your Writing Talent*

- *Who Are You Speaking To*

- *Forming An Audience*

- *Becoming A Showcase Author*

My Testimony:

If I Can You Have No Excuse

It's so much you must know to get you through a successful writing journey and in this book are plenty of strategies. I never thought I would complete as many books as I have. It was hard but I persevered and the more I wrote the more challenges arose. However, I did not let my challenges conquer me with fear because fear makes failures and that is one title I was not willing to wear. Yes, there was so many obstacles that bum rushed

It's Time To Get That Book Out Of You!

my life but through all I birthed one book after another. In writing you must stay focused regardless of what's trying to hinder your progress.

Struggling To Write

A tremendous amount of trials barricaded my life during my writing journey and I kept on pushing that book out of me. It was something awesome being birthed through me as I struggled to write. All kinds of things rose up to challenge the author inside me to be birthed. I would not want my worst enemy to endure any of my past struggles or the enormous weight I had to carry while I wrote. I was tried from every side that caused me to wonder if the word was even true. Let absolutely nothing have the power to cause you to stop because it will be devastating to your life and you will never complete your divine assignment or be able to reach your heart's desires. I tell people you will only get one life so you better make it work while you have it. In my past I may have quit other things but with this one thing,

It's Time To Get That Book Out Of You!

I struggled because my books deserved to live. No one could give your book the right to be birthed but you. Many people laughed at me and do not believe I survived nine strokes. I am the Book Stylist and one that EMPOWERS. My life's purpose is to inspire countless through the grace given to me to motivate conquerors to be more than what they have ever been. For years I thought I was cursed but the enemy did not want me to ever reach you. All that I went through, I decided the best is yet to come. I just decided that strokes and horrific trials were not going to get the best of me. However, I was going to get the best out of my afflictions and make my testimonies owe me severance pay. You can let your pains in life keep you in drought or tap into the power of sufferings and let vision bring you out. Authors are inspired many different ways through sufferings, hardship, neglect, hurt, loss, loneliness, sickness, fear, struggles, inspirations and testimonies. There is a very high percentage of wealthy people that conquered greatly through vision. Something great inspired them and they became the author of their

It's Time To Get That Book Out Of You!

creation. Your book has the power to release everything you ever desired but *The Birth of an Author Shall Be Born* before you can receive them. How Can You Push If You Have Nothing to Birth? It's impossible and only you can push that book out. My books deserve to live, what about yours? If, you have inspiring vision to write you better get started because what good is life without vision. I used to sit and dream what if and for years it remained a question? What if this and what if that? I opened my eyes and realized I had the power to make my dream come to pass but I had to work fervently to make it happen. Eventually, it paid off but there is the only thing that does pay and that is work.

Pushing That Book Out Of You

I tell you the more I grew to write, the more mountains I had to climb. A writer must overcome the depth of their struggles to survive. In their vision are great solutions and that is why authors must write. Vision writers can solve problems in a supernatural way; their vision is the key to others dreams.

It's Time To Get That Book Out Of You!

You will never know the impact of your book until it's complete. One Sunday evening I was invited to speak. As I entered the facility, this worship leader was discussing my book *A Precious Gift From God* and she complimented it extremely well. I did not realize the potential it really had. A Precious Gift From God was the motivation she needed to strengthen her as a worship leader. In addition, she was persuading all to order the book and how great it was. She did not know I was walking up behind her and that is how I heard the conversation. It made me feel like a million bucks. Your book (vision) is the solution to someone else's problem. It's imperative you write your book because there is another vision waiting to be inspired.

Vision Multiplied

During my writing journey I had also envisioned *Fountain of Life Publisher's House,* a place to end an author's nightmare. I laughed but I was greatly moved at the thought of becoming a book publisher. The more I went forth in writing books, the more there was a

It's Time To Get That Book Out Of You!

need for *Fountain of Life Publisher's House* to exist. I was destined to publish other authors. Right now you may just be a writer trying to overcome the struggles of your journey. Who knows the end? You must persevere to find out the potential of the book inside you. Considering a book is a vision and it tells a story that will witness what you envision and will be a great resource for others, Whether it's motivational, how to, or entertaining and inspiring. Regardless, others will be lead in a new direction after reading your book. I remember watching the movie Pursuit of Happiness with Will Smith and his son. We often wonder how others made it but their struggles were never easy and they are there to build up our confidence. It put me in the mind as I lived in hotels that I did not let it stop my writing journey. My health was not good as I had continued to go in and out of hospitals having strokes, which attack the brain. I still did not let it stop me. This movie inspired me and I said, "If he can so can I." Often, many have more than what they need but still won't do anything. Through the years I did not let my struggles stop my

It's Time To Get That Book Out Of You!

writing journey because the more I wrote the more I released. Let nothing have the power over your book and only you can push it out!

The Power of an Author

The power of an author is amazing and how they will astound others. Authors strengthen the minds of others and the health and wealth of countless. The power of an author is limitless. Remember, an author is a writer and a writer writes vision and through vision there is freedom. Your book has the potential to free others. What if I had not written *Living Life In A Messed Up Situation* volume one, then I would never have written *Living Life In A Messed Up Situation* volume two. It was the inspiration of volume one that inspired volume two. The power of an author is deep and has no ending because their minds are always working in expectation to make something happen. An author's eye is bigger than their hope and it's the way they hope that reels in their heart's desire. Once a vision appears to an author it becomes possible and the word *impossible* is not in

It's Time To Get That Book Out Of You!

their vocabulary. Regardless of the amount of time and strenuous efforts an author will make, it happens and their nights will be restless until they begin to see change. Authors are courageous creators and dynamic visionaries even when little to nothing is in their view because they are vision expanders. The power of an author is that they have no limits and allow nothing to stop their perseverance. Once they see vision it's all over and they will not stop until it all comes to pass.

It's Time To Get That Book Out Of You!

The Birth of an Author
Shall Be BORN

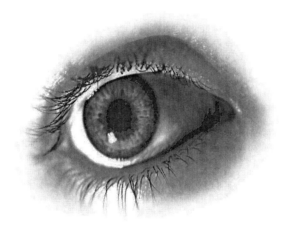

Authors can never give up because if they quit on vision it will never come to pass!

~ Parice Parker

The Birth of an Author

Shall Be BORN

Chapter Two

Finding Time to Write

Finding the time to write is the main excuse writers use not to finish their book. Writing a book can be extremely challenging and it requires a lot of time and great effort to work. Time is really easy to find but you must take a moment to itemize your time.

It's Time To Get That Book Out Of You!

Yes, itemize your time because time is a terrible thing to waste.

Enumerate Your Time

If you sit down and log your time in, you would be amazed at how much time in a day you are wasting. Once you carefully log in per hour and take inventory of your day, then add it up by the week; before you know it, by the end of the year there will be months of wasted time that could have added value to your life. Time sheets are needed because in order to be a successful author there will be great sacrifices and it's time over matter. Make your time count meaning sum up goods for your life. Your time is either investing wealth transfer in your life or deleting your hope of fulfillment. Time is very valuable and too many do not value their time. I too used to be very careless of time. But, one day I refused to lose my dreams of making my visions to become real just because life, at times, grew complicated. I once saw this movie called *In Time* that made something click to be greater. As the lady ran

It's Time To Get That Book Out Of You!

to meet her son she ran out of time. In this movie time mattered and your life depended on time. You could not afford to waste it because once your time ran out your life span expired unless a deposit was being made. It really made me think if I had been broke I would have died. Think of all the time many have wasted when that time could have mounted up to something. As this mother ran she fell into her son's arms. On the spot she died and the saddest part was that he had just received a massive amount of time. They were trying to meet up so he could transfer time to her. All because she did not have enough money to catch the bus she ran out of life's opportunity. Yes, time does matter. I sat there and saw my life flash before my eyes and if I had lived in that movie, plenty of times, I would have died.

Wasted Time Is Irreplaceable

Time is a terrible thing to waste. A writer must find time and replace wasted time with writing. I once told someone fifteen

It's Time To Get That Book Out Of You!

minutes a day (equals one page) multiplied by 365 days a year can get you 1 or more complete books depending on your page count. As I was teaching The Birth of an Author Shall Be Born Creative Writing Workshop, the participants were in AWE when we discussed this. Everyone was in AWE once they realized the possibility of how many books could be written in one year. In writing an author will get dedicated and more serious with their journey because time is of the essence. Finding the time to write is the key to completing your book.

A Distraction Trying to Get You off Point

Television was a big distraction when I first began my writing journey. I found time to write by replacing it with my television time. Once you prove you can dedicate at least fifteen minutes a day then you know you can find more time to write. Time is the key to your endeavor so search for time and rearrange your schedule. As you log in your appointment book, add writing time and submit to it. Sooner than later you will see

It's Time To Get That Book Out Of You!

great progress. In my beginning stage of becoming an author, making dates with my computer was another way I dedicated myself to writing. I took it completely serious. The more time I spent in writing the more my heart yearned to finish. If you add up that television time and the telephone time per day and multiply it by seven days, this would be the weekly time you could afford to transfer too your writing journey. Begin to search every day for time you can replace with writing; this is key to getting the job done. I begin to treat my writing journey as a job even though I was not getting paid at the moment. I just considered it retirement pension but I never quit. I wrote month in and month out even when my books were not selling. I remember seeing this woman on Oprah's show a few years ago. She inspired me though I did not see the beginning of the show and I never knew her name. However, she had written thirteen books and on her thirteenth, she finally made it. I was often mesmerized that if I had to write thirteen books to make it, then I would. I had come this far and I could not turn back now. It was

It's Time To Get That Book Out Of You!

all worth the challenge. It's more challenging afterward writing a book than before completing one . So, therefore, this is the easy part just finding time to write. Turn off the television and radio then click on your computer or iPad but write. Everyday put time in whether it's a few minutes, hours or just a few sentences. It all adds up make your time count. At that time I was on my seventh book. Once a published author you will write more and more. Now, writing is natural to me and no longer complicated. Through my writing journeys I conquered the irritations of completing a book.

Stay On Point

I have seen a lot of people waste a tremendous amount of time networking about nothing on the internet such as chatting. It's a big distraction. You will be easily diverted in another direction and you will drift from your purpose. Time holds the key to your prosperity and what you do with it really matters. Do not waste time conversing in network if it's not profiting you

It's Time To Get That Book Out Of You!

anything. There is one online social network that when I visit people begin to pop up. How is ministry, family and life? Already, they do not want anything but to waste my time. In approaching someone be ready because it's an opportunity for you. If you are not prepared you will lose their interest such as many lost my focus. Professionals are very careful how they use their time and they do not waste it but make it add up. Always stay on point because that is the key to focusing on your goal to complete your book.

The Phone Is a Big Distraction

The most wasted time is in conversations with people that are doing nothing but wasting your time. Twenty minutes could get you three pages or more. Now, imagine all the time wasted on the phone that could be used in writing your new book. The telephone is easy to get caught up in one conversation to the next then it changes your mode. Allow your voice mail to pick up when you are writing. It's a great disturbance. Most conversation is not worth

It's Time To Get That Book Out Of You!

getting caught up in or giving your time up for it. After you are done writing then return calls unless it's an emergency call. There were many times I took a break and answered the phone. I did not complete my assignment that day because I got out of the mode of writing. The worst thing an author can do is be distracted when the flow is going good. It is never good to interrupt your writing but even an author must overcome distractions and let nothing interfere with their deadline to get the book done. I remember as I was working on this one book while traveling back to Atlanta. One person was listening to music and the microphone was so loud I could hear everything. In addition, this child was talking, the air was blasting and I heard over ten others on the phone but I grew desperate to get this book completed. I could not even allow a distraction to stop me. The life I desired had been on hold for so long I grew beyond distractions and still wrote. I realized it was my gift of writing and the book I had to get out was the key to unlock my right now needs. So, therefore distractions who or what? I could not focus on what was going

It's Time To Get That Book Out Of You!

on around me because I had to get it done. I was no longer willing to delay my own prosperity any longer. I was prepared to make every minute of my life count. A big week was a head of me and I had a lot to look forward to. The pressure was on and the writing kicked in. I could not stop or give in to any excuse. I wanted the life that's been promised to me and I could not allow another minute to pass me by because I was too close to my destiny. Once you begin to stop giving your excuse an excuse you will get that book done without making another reason why you do not have time.

Sometime Writing Bores Me

Yes, it's boring sometimes writing but that is when you must let your imagination show you something new such as a dream, fantasy or vision. Your dreams have the potential to keep you motivated that is why you must continue looking forward and pursuing your writing journey. Remember every minute counts and if it's not catapulting you upward then replace that

It's Time To Get That Book Out Of You!

time slot with writing. For years I complained about what I did not have. My freedom was in my books but I had to write them before I could obtain my heart's desires. Each book told a story and had a piece of my destiny but I had to continue. Although I was bored, that's when I received another vision to spark my flame to write. The more I grew lonely the more I begin to accomplish because I had plenty of time to write. Actually, it's the most I have ever accomplished being in a lonely place with no distractions. Loneliness does pay off well when you make your time count it will surely increase your life. Invest in your prosperity with making your time work for you. Prosperity comes as one inherits wealth but all requires work. A lot of people want success but it comes with a big price tag and only time could pay for it. So make every minute count because it's your opportunity to gain that's going down the drain.

Loneliness

I found loneliness to become my best friend after writing quite a few books. The

It's Time To Get That Book Out Of You!

more I wrote the more I grew lonely. It's like everyone disappeared. Make your time count and it will add great value to your life. You cannot inherit something you have not invested in. So do not worry about being lonely because I found good qualities in it. Loneliness cannot distract you, get on your nerves, make a loud noise, take you off focus and interrupt your writing flow. You stay focused when you are lonely so there are some good points about being lonely; it protects your flow. So enjoy loneliness because it protects your writing flow. In addition, it helps you complete your new book.

It's Time To Get That Book Out Of You!

The Birth of an Author Shall Be BORN...

Is it you?

It's Time To Get That Book Out Of You!

The Birth of an Author
Shall Be BORN

A great economic fall is due to aborted visions!

~ Parice Parker

34 *Discover the author in you.*

The Birth of an Author
Shall Be BORN

Chapter Three

My Book Deserves To Live

Only you could feel the heartbeat of your new book. No one can feel the love for your creation as you do. If you cannot get the job done, then do not expect anyone else to. Show others what you see by making your

It's Time To Get That Book Out Of You!

creation visible. The power of your work will cause you to prosper in all areas of life and do not wait on anyone to help you just do it. Give your book life by birthing that book out of you. I hear so many proclaim they are writing a book year in and year out. Often we tend to tell others what we are doing too soon. My mother used to say, "Do not tell all but show all." Simply means keep your mouths shut and get the job done; even the bible tells us do not let the right hand know what the left hand is doing. I found in book writing the best kept secret is being quite until you complete the book because once spoken everything tries to come against you to hinder your progress.

How Do I Start My Book?

The best way to start your book is to allow what's in your heart to just flow. Get a piece of paper and begin to write. I know computers are more convenient but it's something special about a pen and a piece of paper. It strokes the heart of the writer. My first book I begin was *Aggravated Assault on*

It's Time To Get That Book Out Of You!

Your Mind and, of course, I did not know it was going to be a book. I was angry that day and all fed up. I had a house full of guests. A few were living with me. My husband and I always tried to help people but this time I grew to a boiling point. I was so angry I wanted to fight but I knew that was out of the question. Nevertheless, I wanted them out of my house but I knew that would be mean. So I heard a voice and it said, "Write out your anger." I begin to release every thought to a piece of paper with the tips of a pen. One word came after another everything just flowed together. Once I finished, I went inside the house and begin to read aloud to my husband. Afterwards, I told him this was how I felt. He asked, "Where is the book." I begin to get angry again because I felt he was not listening. After writing out my anger I grew calm and it relieved the tension. However, he still questioned me about the book because he wanted to read it. Now, if I would have not listened the book would have never been written. He thought what I had read was good and afterwards he was convinced it was already a book but he did not know I was the author. So I received it. I needed to write this book and every time I read the introduction to *Aggravated Assault on Your Mind* to someone, they wanted to immediately purchase the book. On that evening a whole new chapter of my life began because I began my true writing journey. It was a great relief because years prior I always told people I am going to write a book and I finally got started.

The Flow in Your Heart

Find out what is in your heart and once you recognize your passion to write you will begin to flow. I am an inspirational author; that's what flows out of me. It's a strength I have and I was born with it. You have to know your flow in writing to be successful. One day I was looking at a television show and they were talking about Steven King's project, Carrie. I believe this was his first but once he had completed it he threw it in the trash. You would be amazed how successful you can become as an author. Yes, Steven King is an exceptional author in creating

It's Time To Get That Book Out Of You!

movies. He gets deep in the mind and the movies many see comes from books. An author is a creator and we invent what we see. Whether its books, movies, objects, plays, things, toys and stuff. Everything in this world has an author including the car you ride in, the house you're live in and the companies you have worked for. All are authors; it's someone's dream and vision that they brought to pass. There is a flow in your heart and you must write it out. It is something how Steven King trashed one of his biggest hits because he did not think it was good enough. It's a good thing he did not leave it there.

I'm writing a Book

A lot of people want to be an author but you can only be one once your work is published. At this point you are just a writer and you must set a time on your graduation. Give yourself a date to complete your book; it will help you plan for success. What if Steven King would have still been telling people I'm going to make a movie called Carrie? He

It's Time To Get That Book Out Of You!

would have not had all the success he has if he would have still been talking and not working. In addition, all the other movies that came because of his endeavors would have never been birthed. Success requires hard work. Once you complete your book or begin on one, another will come to mind. Ideas come when your mind is at work. Although *Aggravated Assault on Your Mind* was the first book I started, it was not my first I completed and published.

No Excuse

Living Life in a Messed up Situation Volume One was my first published book. All my writings were inspired by God and there is a push behind every title. One day I went to church after losing a lot being a Pastor and not having my own things. This will make you feel worthless. This Sunday morning I went to visit this other church in Charlotte, NC, my home town, and I sat in the very back of the church. I did not want anyone to recognize me. I just needed a WORD. The Bishop came to the mike and said, "God don't

It's Time To Get That Book Out Of You!

bless no mess!" I looked as I was startled and replied in my heart, "YES HE DOES!" Immediately I heard the voice of the Lord commissioned me to get up and tell the world that He specialized in blessing those *Living Life in a Messed up Situation.* If not even I do not serve a purpose. He told me to tell the world because too many have preached that wrong. Once I arrived home after leaving church early I went straight to my office and was driven with a great passion to complete a book I had not started. I finished that book in seven days. So there is no excuse why you have not completed your book or a chapter or a sentence. A purpose must drive your heart to write.

The Drive of Your Heart to Write

The drive of your heart is your stirring wheel to your destiny. My drive was correction to inspire truth to be revealed. I write what moves me so I can touch someone else and empower a move in them. Everyone that wants to be an author is not because everyone cannot explain through work what

It's Time To Get That Book Out Of You!

they see. An author is not a talker but a worker of creation. An author moves through passion to see their end and to be inspired to create more. Our minds never stop designing. There is always a detail to connect a simple dot to your next paragraph or sentence in your book but you must complete one paragraph before you go to the next. Only you can explain to the world what you see through the creation of your work. Each book I have written has a purpose to empower others in their mission. The titles speak to the reader to inquire within and once they pick it up they purchase. As you are driven to write your title will become clear and will give you drive to continue writing your book. Thinking back when I had my beauty salon one of my clients asked me the question. "What's in your heart?" Time stood still for a moment as I pondered me standing on a platform empowering others to succeed and being a successful author. At the time I was writing like crazy I could not control the writing. Books were flowing out of my heart left and right. You have to know what's in your heart and then want it bad enough. So

It's Time To Get That Book Out Of You!

much until you will no longer be complacent because it's either this life you are living or it's the one you dream. I chose my dream life; that is the power of an author, they are creators.

Speaking to the Heart of a Writer

I know you may feel you cannot achieve this journey because of your previous history of quitting something. I'm here to tell you YES YOU CAN! I never knew I would become who I am but I am because I decided to move out of where I was and who I used to be. Yes, this journey will be difficult but you can overcome. Look at your past; all the other challenges. Your overcoming this one is no greater because they all require work. You want a new life, make a move from this one and let nothing interfere with your writing flow. Get serious and acquaint yourself with who you are purposed to become. The more you ask yourself, "Where do I begin," the more you will allow yourself not to complete your assignment. A great tip to writing is to begin and the more you write the more you

It's Time To Get That Book Out Of You!

will be driven to write. One thing about an author is that they become lonely people so eventually the excuses are no longer excuses. Just start and keep writing. Eventually, you will have a finished book.

It's Time To Get That Book Out Of You!

The Birth of an Author
Shall Be BORN

The Author stimulates the eye and has the capability of birthing visionaries.

~ Parice Parker

The Birth of an Author

Shall Be BORN

Chapter Four

Overcoming Writers Block

Overcoming writers' block is sometimes complicated but I know the secrets to writers' block. Authors often just get stuck and cannot write no matter how hard they will try. Taking breaks can be crucial in the beginning stages of writing because

It's Time To Get That Book Out Of You!

temptation sneaks in along with becoming slothful. You must treat your writing assignment like a job because if you do not complete your book you cannot get paid. I often say many rob their own prosperity by cheating themselves the opportunity to strive for greater. Every missed opportunity is a waste of time. Begin to prepare this journey as the best business deal you will ever make. Put the best effort in your new book and you will finish sooner than you think. I have never seen one that strive towards Excellency not succeed because as long as you are trying it will happen.

The First Secret to Overcoming Writers Block

The main reason writers' block occurs is the author is not staying focused in writing and they are not writing enough. The more you write the more a writer is geared to write. Obtaining a continuous writing journey is vital. It influences more to come out of you and incorporates additional vision. You will be able to see more and further plus

It's Time To Get That Book Out Of You!

clearer. It allows you to see the next step and that is what gives you the extra boost to move forward. The key to overcoming writers' block is to write more and do not give in to breaking periods. I have seen a breaking period turn into years that was only going to be minutes or days. A break invites laziness, lack of work, tiredness and fatigue to overtake you and they are never good when beginning to write. Breaks are hazardous to authors because they will delay or postpone your production of work. The old saying no work no pay and that includes completion of work.

Remove Things/People from Your Life

It may sound harsh but something or someone is bringing continuous interruption in your life. It's hard for you to stay focused. It's time you chose what's more important. The book inside you or that which postponed your progress; the choice is yours. If you do not get serious about writing your book and stay focused no one else will. I notice when the writing gets good, everything tries to

It's Time To Get That Book Out Of You!

hinder my progress but I have learned some secrets in writing. As you read, I will share those secrets but no one is changing my sleep time. I sacrificed by going to bed earlier when I'm writing so I can have private time to write myself. During the middle of the night I rarely have had to deal with distractions or interruptions.

The Second Secret to Overcoming Writers Block

Perhaps there is a twin to your book meaning another book is being birthed. It will happen as you write. A whole new book will come to your mind and it may be that book that brings excitement to your writing journey. It has happened to me plenty of times. As I was working on *Aggravated Assault on Your Mind* the fourth book came to mind. I had a new book which was *A Precious Gift from God.* This book gave me an extra writing boost. It speaks to the heart of the leaders. As I visited many churches the same thing was happening. The leader inside did not realize the power of their gifts. Though they were utilizing them they did not fully

It's Time To Get That Book Out Of You!

understand the value and how precious the gift was. I was motivated to write what God had inspired me to write. Just think if I would have just stayed on the one book *Aggravated Assault on Your Mind* then I would have missed out on 3 or more titles. Truly, I had written more than I could have imagined as I work on one. The more you write the more you will look further ahead and when see what's in your view it will excite you.

Book Scraps

Often you will begin to write completely out of context with what you previously had. I consider it scraps for your book but great material for another. Throw away nothing - soon your scraps will measure up. It's important to stay on point in writing to help the flow of your book speak to the heart of your reader. Make sure you keep an open file to store your scraps. What's insignificant in your current book will be visible for another. Just cut and paste. I have had scraps amount up to an entire book. Be

It's Time To Get That Book Out Of You!

willing to waste nothing not even your scraps.

Tips To Save Your Book

Secrets I use to back up my files and some very helpful tips. It is good to email your files to yourself so if you ever lose your computer or get a virus your files will be backed up. It's the easiest and cost absolutely nothing. Open a new email just for your book and each time you write email the file to yourself. You can still have a flash drive but its best to back up more than one way. So you won't lose your work. I have lost quite a few books I was working on and some were finished. It will save you a lot of time.

Record & Be Ready

A writer's mind is always at work even when they are not writing. Be ready for great ideas that will surface in weird places, at odd moments and when you least expect them to. Often when I'm cooking something comes to mind and I like to keep my voice recorder

It's Time To Get That Book Out Of You!

near so I will not miss the opportunity. I used to say I will remember and always forgot. So I learned to prepare myself not to lose the opportunity of losing a good thought. It could be titles for a book, a topic to write on, a title for a chapter or the hook I have been waiting for. However, I learned many lessons overcoming many losing battles. One thought is not worth losing because it could be your golden thought. Make sure you keep a voice recorder ready at all times. It's easier to record than write because you can forget what to write while writing it down. Altogether, every thought is worth recording because it could substantially increase the sales of your book and cause the greatest award to be granted to you. So therefore no thought is worth deleting or missing out on recording. Often, good thoughts will spontaneously come to mind and then in a blink of an eye it's gone. Thoughts are the creation of multiplication because one thought increases another. There have been many times I have had something good in my mind but as soon as the phone rings and I answer the thought disappears. Also, times I

It's Time To Get That Book Out Of You!

said that I will remember but did not write it down, soon afterwards the thought was gone. Thoughts are patterns to complete your destiny and every thought is worth recording even the ones you delete.

Recording that Thought

This is where you can also put old phones back to work. The majority of phones have a voice recorder. Use them to be on point when a book idea arrives in your head. Record everything because it could be the most important part of your book and never say I will remember because you will forget. I have lost great thoughts because I did not prepare myself. Keep a note pad and plenty of pens in your needed areas. These places are the best places to be ready and keep prepared for a thought to surface. The bathroom is a good place for thoughts to arrive, the kitchen, patio, den and your nightstand when you wake up in weird hours with a thought. Also stay ready in the car - a very good place for thoughts to surface but you must stay ready.

It's Time To Get That Book Out Of You!

The Third Secret to Overcoming Writers' Block

You must keep your mind inspired with book writing. A lot of people do not invest in their own inspirations. As you are writing go out and invest in other books because the more you read the more you will be inspired to write. Thoughts are collective information points that are stimulated from a point of interest. So, therefore, if you are working on a cook book the more you invent new dishes and practice is the more you will write about how to cook. I am an inspirational author so I love to stay inspired with positive people, positive things plus motivational speakers. My spirit must be fed with great motivation in order to release inspirations. Be careful what you let enter your mind because it will produce your life. I am also very careful who I connect with. If they are negative I will be drained and not able to be inspiring to others. I love to read and listen to great inspirational speakers because they help me stay motivated to accomplish my task. Get to know other

It's Time To Get That Book Out Of You!

authors and read their books. It will help generate you to become a more effective author.

The Fourth Secret to Overcoming Writers' Block

Write what you know because you have the keys to solving problems by sharing hidden truths in you. You must know what kind of author you are because you must obtain the focus of your readers in order to keep their attention span. There are many authors but are the books serving a good purpose in fulfilling its obligation to the reader? Your book must fulfill its purpose or it will not sell and you must stay focused on explaining key points in your new book. Get to know what kind of author you are and operate in your strengths to fulfill your readers and your authors audience will grow. *The Birth of an Author Shall Be Born* is to motivate the author inside to discover their destined creative work. In addition, as I was writing this book I saw a need to do more 'how to write book seminars' titling it as *The*

It's Time To Get That Book Out Of You!

Birth of An Author Shall Be Born. Plus, I also saw a need to send this book to every author that published with our company simply because it contains valuable information that every writer and soon to be author needs. *The Birth of An Author Shall Be Born* has limitless opportunities and I want them all. Out of one idea a continuous creative work flowed countless ways to market *The Birth of An Author Shall Be Born.* However, if I would have quit because my previous books did not hit record breaking sales, I would have stayed in a complacent state of mind. I would have had no growth and missed opportunities because I would have stopped at a point that was not my breaking point. To overcome writer's block you must never stop writing regardless of how many books you have previously written. Never quit trying to get that New York Times Best Seller Book out of you.

It's Time To Get That Book Out Of You!

The Birth of an Author
Shall Be BORN

An author gives sight to the blind!

~ Parice Parker

The Birth of an Author Shall Be BORN

Chapter Five

Placing My Chapters

I do not know how to place my chapters is such a familiar statement. I tell writers if you have a book inside that deserves to live you will get it out because

It's Time To Get That Book Out Of You!

your spirit will become restless. Placing chapters is the least of your worries. It is a question to keep the excuses around. As long as there is an excuse there will be no book. Most people that ask this question have not even written one chapter. Now, why be concerned about placing chapters you have not written yet. Your duty is to write and as you continue one chapter opens another. It is hard placing something that does not exist yet, believe me. When you finish one chapter another will complement the previous chapter. Your book has been, held up long enough, just begin to clock in and go to work in writing your new book.

The Title

Your book title is the worm of the fisherman's hook. It lures people to the book and once they bite the rest begins to real them in such as book cover, introduction and back insert. One word or more is the statement of your book and it is the attraction to the reader. It must speak in print boldly to make one inquire within. *Aggravated Assault on*

It's Time To Get That Book Out Of You!

Your Mind is a very luring title and it covers the entire content of the book. All complement one another from the book cover design, introduction, back insert, book contents, chapter titles and tag catches (I Can't Take One More Thing). It's also good to share the response of your titles with friends or getting family opinions are always good because you learn from them. What may sound good to you may sound awful to them. It's always good to see the reactions of others because what matters is that your book sells. This book is titled *The Birth of An Author Shall Be Born* and as you are reading this book it's empowering the author in you to want to come out. Now, for years, I knew I'd soon write this book but I wanted the title to be, *Get That Book out of you* but instead, I used that as my catch tag. *The Birth of An Author Shall Be Born* burned in my heart for years. I also named my seminars for creative writing *The Birth of An Author Shall Be Born*. There was such a great need for me to teach writing tips and give helpful hints because people were always asking me for help in book

It's Time To Get That Book Out Of You!

writing. I started my seminar and book tour even before the book was written.

The Purpose of an Author

A true author is a great listener; their ears are the eyes that see what the ears need to hear. We listen as we watch television and we hear as our eyes see. An author's mind never rest because they are always in a creative mode. They never fit in and always feel left out and alone because there is something unique about an author. Most of the times they are un-happy because they are in a world they do not belong. Authors have uniqueness about them but most cannot pinpoint the problem because their solutions are in their work. Most authors are very problematic people because they must form their world to come. No one has the power over that key but them and the world they desire is inside them. It must be birthed through their work ethic of birthing their vision to come to past. Everything that exists in this world had an author, such as your car, house, table, chair, cell phone, pen, computer,

It's Time To Get That Book Out Of You!

and utensils. If you can touch it and its tangible there is an author whose work was once a vision until they birthed it into existence. There would be no knowledge if it was not for authors, or inventors, hospitals, doctors, schools, lawyers, library, bookstores, and more. Authors exist to create and if we do not operate in our divine assignment we prolong our own unhappiness and misery. An author's joy is in the fruit of their labor and the happiness in a finished product of their work. Authors are missioned for purposed and until our mission is complete our inheritance cannot be transferred. My book, *The Anointing Powers of Your Hands,* represents the power of creation in ones hands. We all have the power to create because *The Anointing Powers of Your Hands* can bring forth amazing results if you put them to better use. I hear complaints about life but all they need to do is exercise The Anointing Powers in their hands. The power of an author has no boundaries just get that book out of you and your limits will be removed.

It's Time To Get That Book Out Of You!

The Catch is what Hooks

The catch is the inspiration of the sale that continues to stimulate the buyer. It's the guide to attract the eye and gives it power to pull the reader in. Once the reader is pulled in and begins inquiring about the book other things begin to pressure the reader to purchase. The catch has the power to win the readers' heart. I consider it purchasing power. Make sure your catch has the power to shape the mind of the buyer and motivate you to gain a new reader because the best advertisement is by word of mouth.

Book Cover

Your book cover identifies what's inside your book. It is the face to the book content and it's the number one thing that catches the eye. If you can catch the attention of an eye you might make a sale. Make sure your cover speaks for your book. My book, *Living Life in a Messed Up Situation volume one,* represents hardship so I was led to use a brick wall as my cover page. It speaks to

It's Time To Get That Book Out Of You!

every heart with bricks. I chose bricks because many get backed into a wall or it's hard to bulldoze a brick wall without enough push and the right bulldozer. You need heavy gear to bust through a brick wall and it also represents *Living Life in a Messed up Situation volume one*. Your cover design must have a drawing effect to attract readers. Once the reader picks up the book then the next place they go is to the introduction or the back insert. It's a fifty- fifty flip that's why your back also must be explosive. The book cover must influence the eye of the reader to take interest of your book and once they inquire the next focus should pull in the sale.

Back Insert

The shaping of the book sale is in the back insert. It should induce the mind where there's no putting that book down. I have seen it both ways. Once a person of interest picks up the book they would go to the introduction or to the back insert. Most just glance through the introduction but they read the back of the book. It's the attention grabber

It's Time To Get That Book Out Of You!

because that's the power to seduce the reader. The back insert must have an effect on the reader to hunger for more. One of my greatest back insets that has always sold on my book was *this book is like the coldest and sweetest cup of Kool-Aide on the hottest summer day of my life.* After losing all I had, *Living Life in a Messed up Situation Volume One* was the beginning of discovering the author in me. There was a need to soothe the hurt, pain, and loss of all who were living life in a messed up situation. I only had one person to put it down but 99% purchased the book once they read the back insert. Your back insert is your fastener so make it such that it presses the sale of the book. Just as stylist need clients you need readers; they are going to be your customers, fans and book supports so keep them nailed through the attention of your books.

The Power of an Introduction

Your Introduction needs to be explosive! It's the greatest pull for the reader. Once a reader takes interest in a book the next

It's Time To Get That Book Out Of You!

place is the introduction. If the introduction grips the heart of the reader a sale is made. Regardless of whether they ever read the rest of the book, the introduction pegs the sale. Your introduction is the summary of your book. It will be the guide for the writer if the introduction is written in the beginning? Also, it's the complete summary if the introduction is written at the end of the book. Some of my book introductions came in the beginning and then some as I completed the book. Others I have revised after the book was written. You have to be in the right mode to write the introduction because this is the part of the book your heart, mind and soul must be led to persuade the heart of the reader. Often I have tried writing my introduction with all the right thoughts but my heart was not in it. Your soul must feel it as your heart is being led by the captivating of your mind. A writer will express through utilizing their talents. If the reader cannot feel the mode of your book there will be no interest. As you write speak to the heart of your reader and make sure they feel the sensation of your book. Open your heart and

It's Time To Get That Book Out Of You!

pour into words making your book expressible. No fish hook no bait and no bait no catch.

Chapter Titles

Arousing a writer's spirit is to interest the reader with stimulating chapter titles will captivate the reader for a period of time in paragraphs and pages that create a chapter? The title of your chapter needs to fulfill the name of the title chapter. It must keep the attention of the reader to go to the next chapter. Chapter titles fasten the mind to desire more. It makes a mind hunger such as *The Anointing Powers of Your Hands,* one of my stimulating books to read; another great seller. The chapter titles are as follows: *1) Press And Push, 2) Fighting the Battle - Defeating Your Giant, 3) The Heart of Your Hands Beating At Work, 4) Spiritual Inflammation, 5) Praying To The Point Of No Return, 6) Seven Keys To Prayer, 7) Getting To Know Your Hands Personality, 8) Finger Out Your Faith; 9) Allowing The Milk & Honey To Flow In Your Life.* See how one chapter

It's Time To Get That Book Out Of You!

compliments the other. It makes a huge difference and a great impact on the potential reader. The chapters are counter parts of the book title *The Anointing Powers of Your Hands* and have the ability to fulfill the need of the buyer. The more an author writes the more they are geared to create.

It's Time To Get That Book Out Of You!

The Birth of an Author
Shall Be BORN

If evidence is not your end result then, what good is your effort?

~ Parice Parker

The Birth of an Author

Shall Be BORN

Chapter Six

Finalizing Your Book for Print

Yes, there are a few things you need to know to prepare your book for print. Once you have read over your book once or twice then leave it alone because you will find yourself changing your entire book. As I once

It's Time To Get That Book Out Of You!

stated creative thoughts multiply ones thinking and the more you read over your book the more changes you will begin to make. Once you have read over your book it is time for a new set of eyes to view your book. A few things to check for making sure your titles, chapters and paragraphs compliment one another. Your final read is preparing your new book for the editor's eye. Also recheck to see if you have the following:

> Content page
> Introduction or preface
> Acknowledgments
> A brief biography
> Any signed agreements for statements or permission of use
> Your hook that goes on the back of your book
> Your Chapters Are In Place
> A back up file
> Endorsement

Choosing Your Book Publisher

Choosing a book publisher can be complicated but first you want to pick one

It's Time To Get That Book Out Of You!

that gives you freedom to still be the author. There are different kinds of book publishers and they have their own way of publishing operation. Choose one that can give you an opportunity to be expressive and help you develop to be a better author. Every author has big dreams to be the next New York Times Best seller and it is possible but you must plan big. Set your goals to be big and write down a good plan to be a successful author. Yes, marketing is a plus and that is the difference between a POD (Print-on-Demand) book publisher and a traditional book publisher.

Traditional Book Publisher

Nowadays, you must prove yourself before a traditional book publisher will notice you since there are so many authors. A lot of authors had to self-publish before they were noticed by a large publishing house. Traditional book publishers offer authors an advance on acceptance of a manuscript. However, your advance may be $10,000.00 and they may not produce the book until a

It's Time To Get That Book Out Of You!

year or two later. Nevertheless, all the money they invest in your book they will begin to subtract from your advance. If they overspend their budget to produce your book, e.g., at $25,000.00 you are paying the cost. Once your book is released it may hit breaking sales or it could be a loss and if the sales do not break even with the cost of your book production then the book will soon stop printing. Yes, you are the author but you sold your rights to sell your book to the publisher that gave you an advance. So therefore most traditional book publishers do not allow their authors to sell. And, once your new book stops printing that is it for that work it is now history. Traditional book publishers have the upper hand on your book publishing services and the way your book sells. After the printing is stopped you have no rights to reprint and if their cost of production is not met then you do not get any more money. Yes, it is very good once your name is big then your advance will also be big. Some of our prominent authors get hundreds, thousands, and millions in advance but you must develop your name to get recognition.

It's Time To Get That Book Out Of You!

Name Recognitions Works:

Building your name is the most difficult thing that is why your plan must be good. One right move is all you need and one right connection can promote you to an entire new class of life. Your name has value but you must identify the gold that is in you. Bishop T D Jakes, Myles Monroe, Joel Olsteen, Stephen King and so many more were unrecognized until they became published authors. In addition, whatever their hands touched is blessed. Most importantly they too once were unpublished and unestablished authors until they made the step to get published. Your gold is within you but you must get it out. Let nothing or anyone come in between your writing journey because you will not experience the fullness until you complete your first book. After you complete your first book then other steps will be given, more ideas will surface and the next book will spring forth.

POD Book Publisher:

It's Time To Get That Book Out Of You!

Print on Demand book publishers is the way many authors publish today and it's a growing trend. Authors are more able to guide their book publishing process because they keep their rights to sell and promote their work. In addition, they can continue to reproduce their book for the length of time they want. Print on demand is also good because it stops printing overages canceling out book returns from unsold books taking a loss. Authors have found it is easier this way. A lot of authors have received great name recognition through self-publishing that also led them to greatness.

It's Time To Get That Book Out Of You!

The Birth of an Author

Shall Be BORN

The power of an author's eye releases life or death!

~ Parice Parker

It's Time To Get That Book Out Of You!

The Birth of An Author
Shall Be BORN

Chapter Seven
The Heart of The Author

It takes years, months, weeks, and days to write a book. However, the choice is yours and it depends on your determination. You must put your heart to work. An author's dedication to completing a book is priceless and often still does not break even.

It's Time To Get That Book Out Of You!

Regardless of the effort and long hours spent working on your book, it is still not promised to be successful. So many authors get turned around because of high expectations for high sales during their first book. I do not know what book you will write that is going to be your great hit. Do not give up if your first, second or third book is not a great success. It takes time. The key to writing a best seller comes a few different ways. Building relations with people in the industry is where you want to be. This will help you gain recognition to your name as an author. You must build a reputation for becoming a good and famous author. Your first book may or may not be a great success but it's your effort that counts. Continuously make time to enhance your marketing skills. Yes, there are great authors with a well-known reputation of being *New York Times Best Selling Authors* and it came with a hefty price. Being in the right place at the right time with the right person will contribute to your success. Nora Roberts is one that has had a tremendous amount of success in writing books. She has written well over 80 books. In order to

It's Time To Get That Book Out Of You!

continue being successful, even a successful writer must keep writing. The more you write the more you are graced to write and the easier writing becomes. Nora Roberts was born to write and her success has been award winning. No matter what a New York Times Best Seller writes, most of the time it will be an overnight sensation. You must build your name to be known as a famous author. Sure, television helps but there are other ways to begin, such as marketing your new book.

Building Your Name

It is time to use what you have. Your name is the key to how great you can become and it's time to build your name. Every person you come into contact with could be your new reader and every one you by pass could have been. Yes, it seems easy but it's really hard getting your name out there unless you know some good tips. One tip that really works is greeting strangers with a compliment and smile. Remember, anyone could be your next potential reader that can also become a great fan that will surely

It's Time To Get That Book Out Of You!

advertise your name as well as your book or books. So do not be so quick to judge just smile and greet. You never know the possibility of an acquaintance until you meet and begin conversation. Not all are going to be kind but you cannot let that stop you. Once your book goes to the market it's time to sell and anyone could be your greatest opportunity to fame or your step in the right connection. Regardless of where you meet a person you never know who they are connected to. Anybody could be that somebody with your next move upward. It's time to get creative and be prepared to miss absolutely no opportunity. Once you strike the conversation and you see it going well make sure you introduce yourself and give them a card. Yes, business cards are the way to impress and make sure your card speaks with a great impression. It has the power to fix a fine connection. Most people do not remember one another just in conversation but they can always reflect back on your business card and contact you. Another thing they will have your information how to purchase your books online or a name to

It's Time To Get That Book Out Of You!

search for more information on the web.
Building your name on a personal basis is a
good way to begin promotions. I will never
forget one night I was watching a television
talk show and the commentator said, "Who
best to promote you but you?" Once you
begin to open your mouth it will be filled
with the things you desired. If people do not
know you exist they cannot support you. So,
therefore, begin to build your name in your
surrounding area with promotional items,
book signing, speaking engagements and
more just as friendly conversation can help
promote you. Always keep business cards
and never run out. Leave some cards in
beauty salons, barber shops where ever
someone will allow you because a potential
new reader may be where you are not and
your business card or post card can draw
them in. There are so many different ways to
build your name and all you have to do is get
started. I will never forget when I opened my
beauty salon, my goal was to target one
thousand people a week with just fliers alone.
So I would get up extra early on Saturdays
and put them on peoples' doors. It boosts my

It's Time To Get That Book Out Of You!

business on Saturdays and it spread my name like crazy. People use to wonder why I was so successful in business but I built my name and once people recognize your talents your name will be reputable. People cannot refer someone they cannot recognize and building your name builds up that good recognition. Soon people will attract more because of word of mouth. Do not despise small beginnings because we all must start somewhere.

Invest For Success You Are Going To Market

Make sure you take the time to build your name because upon becoming a published author you have now become a commodity. I know it may sound harsh but it's true. You have something to market and if you do not sell your book, you will gain nothing. Business cards are a plus because you never know when you or the person you are speaking with is in a hurry. You can pass along a business card in a second and they will have your information. Perhaps, you

It's Time To Get That Book Out Of You!

may run into someone familiar but they do not know of your success and your business card is your presentation. Many of times I missed many good opportunities because I was not prepared or too cheap to invest in business cards or promotional items but I found out that they pay for themselves. One five hundred pack of business cards will pay for itself and reach five hundred new potential buyers. Once a person said, "In business be business" and it took me years of failing experiences to grow to that. I found that to be so true. Prepare to be more successful by investing in your own prosperity. Another way is fliers and post cards. Investing in you pays off when it comes to promotional tools. Set yourself a goal each week on how much attention you want to draw. Get more determined in building your name. Make your name appear everywhere. It is okay to drown out one area of building your name recognition until your name begins to boost sales. Every week for a while I hit the same areas back to back; people had to start checking out who I was. Sometimes people called and said, "I just

It's Time To Get That Book Out Of You!

wanted to meet you because I keep getting these post cards" and then I had the opportunity to let them know my next event. Whether it is a book signing, speaking engagement or book release continue to be ready to share new opportunity. In addition, it's a good way to offer specials and incentives. Keep your name growth on the rise, and continue spreading your name with all sorts of promotional items. I remember when I worked for this make-up company they taught us to pass out at least 20 or more business cards a day and through the years I say keep at least fifty on you at all times. I also passed out at least five hundred or more promotional items a week and it's a good way to get family involved with a great walk. As you hit neighborhoods or parking lots with post cards you can also get your daily exercise and is a great way to expand family time plus prosperity. Make sure you add your marketing tools in your monthly budget and you should always increase as you promote and not decrease.

Forming an Audience

It's Time To Get That Book Out Of You!

Once you recognize your reader base then you will master the art of forming your audience. You will solve the problem of their emptiness, fill the need to their void or just entertain their thought of mind. However, before you can form an audience you must know your genre. Your passion of interest is where you will be more beneficial to your audience or building your reader base. Myles Munroe is an excellent motivational author, speaker and visionary. His life experiences of how he excelled speaks for itself with inspiring books such as: The Purpose and Power of Women, Understanding the Purpose and Power of Prayer, and one of my favorites, In Pursuit of Purpose. He has written over 23 books and most are *Best Sellers* but what if he would have quit once he wrote his first book. Book writing is a creative assignment that highlights views points to direct others in the direction they need to go. Once you find your highlighted creative work then you will find your purpose and build your audience.

Your Name Matters

It's Time To Get That Book Out Of You!

Where is THE BOOK? Where you come from is where your gold is. Mine was through hard tribulation and valleys of numerous trials. I once remember seeing Joel Olsteen with tears flowing down his cheeks when he shared his testimony that he never imagined he could have gained all he has. His titles are inspirational because inspirations are what flow from his heart. He has a passion to make others smile and he operates in Excellency of writing books to inspire people. An author can only express what's in their heart. Joel Olsteen's book, Become a Better You has sold over two million copies. He is a self-help author and now anything with his name on it is a best seller.

History Matters

What if Alex Haley would have never written the book, *Roots*, then look at how many mouths were feed just because of his ambition to write. After looking at the movie again, I was inspired by the gentle man that served with him and requested he write his letters. What if Alex Haley would have not

It's Time To Get That Book Out Of You!

accepted his request? Honoring his request set him up to gain experience in writing. It also woke up a passion to drive into his Divine Purpose and as he was driven in purpose to gather all the information he could about his family history, he also wrote the best novel in history and stirred many to want the movie produced. For centuries Roots have caused countless to press for better. Haley is also *Best* known for The Pulitzer Prize-winning author of the *book* Roots. *Alex Haley wrote* the book Roots, the most prolific novels of the 1970s. You never know the potential inside you until you commit to put your best foot forward. Alex Haley searched in many areas for his purpose and becoming such an inspiring writer his heart was driven to tell the story of his roots. He also spent time being a ghost writer and then wrote the autobiography of Malcolm X that was also a great hit. I often wonder if he would not have discovered the author in him, there would be a lot of untold history that he published.

It's Time To Get That Book Out Of You!

The Birth of An Author
Shall Be BORN

Show the world what the heart of your eyes see.

~ Parice Parker

The Birth of An Author
Shall Be BORN

Chapter Eight

Chasing After What Matters To You

The best advice that I have given returned more favorably was to follow your heart. So many miss life changing opportunities simply because they burned out in life, stopped dreaming and gave up. If you do not keep your desire in front of you then your dreams will never come true. In addition, if you do not continue the up keep

It's Time To Get That Book Out Of You!

of feeding your hope then your dreams will die. A man without vision shall perish. Keep chasing after what matters to you regardless of how fooled you look to others. Keep chasing after all your dreams and soon they will be in your review mirror.

The Power of Your Message

Listening with your heart to hear what motivates you to run. Every runner needs a race and a purpose to run but one must be fit for the journey. Life has a strange way of equipping us for our life journey but we must pay attention to what life is speaking to us. Through the years I heard the voice of many speaking greatness about what they see in me and others inspiring me to go further. People are put in your life for good reason and sometimes even if the intentions are wrong there's still a message for you. Listen to life because life is speaking your next direction. In order to chase after what matters you need to know your direction and be prepared not to miss an opportunity when it knocks.

Chasing Matters

It's Time To Get That Book Out Of You!

The power of the author in you deserves to live but only you have the power to push that author out! What if Face Book did not exist many relationships would have never formed or businesses taken off in the manner they have. What if Alex Haley would not have written Roots we would not have the opportunity of seeing such great history? And, what if our LORD would have never said "Let There Be Light"... there is power that grants opportunity in you! But, the question is whose Opportunity Are You Causing to be delayed because you have not completed your creative work assignment? *The Birth of An Author Shall Be Born* – is it you?

What is your purpose serving?

I heard Bruce Lee say in an interview, "You better train every part of your body". I am reminded that building something bigger than you has never been accomplished. You must tone your entire being to be confident in the completion of your work. Imagine if you were a coffee cup. You can hold all sorts of drink - just a fine example of serving a

It's Time To Get That Book Out Of You!

purpose. A plastic cup will melt if the drink is too hot but a coffee cup can serve more purpose. Nevertheless, if a cup is cracked it will leak out. If it's broken you can pour nothing in. So, therefore, you must build yourself an area to tone your weak area in writing, marketing and gaining recognition. Your work is only as important as you make it. The percentage you put in is the investment you will receive. There is a powerful author in you. Yes, chase what matters and apprehend your dreams. Go bigger, think bigger and be bigger. No one can make it happen like you can.

When You Are Running You Don't Stop

I traded my TV shows and swapped them for a purpose. Every time I wanted to look at TV I wrote in a book, then I completed it. When my BUSINESS ENDED I was able to MAKE MONEY from book sales. Imagine what you can accomplish when you FIND THE TIME TO WRITE!

1) Write 30 Minutes A Day

It's Time To Get That Book Out Of You!

2) Discipline Yourself To Finish One Chapter
A Week
3) Take Your Book On TOUR
4) Increase Your Wealth & Get In Control Of
Your Life.

The BEST Life EXPERIENCE is when you can
really LIVE A GOOD PRODUCTIVE and
healthy life. Time and chance happen to all
but the key is to be ready for your
opportunity. You better be ready for your
opportunity.

Make It Happen For You

The greatest failures are the greatest
successors. After putting your heart in your
new book the real life begins. If no one
believes in you all will fail that is why you
must keep your own hope alive. Be creative
in marketing you because without passion to
excel you will not make it. Passion is
something you drive with force and a set-
mind not to return void. Make sure you gain
from your work with getting a plan to
conquer. There are many ways to get your

It's Time To Get That Book Out Of You!

new book noticed and we will discuss this in the last chapter. Although you are determined to complete your book, once finished, you still need to push your new book. If you don't, do not expect anyone else too. It's time to introduce you to the world with branding your name.

It's Time To Get That Book Out Of You!

The Birth of An Author
Shall Be BORN

A true visionary never dies they visualize.

~ Parice Parker

The Birth of An Author
Shall Be Born

Chapter Nine
The Birthing of Fulfillment:

I remember Mrs. Burton called as I was riding on Buford Highway in Georgia. I pulled over because she had a lot going on and just wanted to get her book published. She began to share the history of her searching for book publishers and it was a

It's Time To Get That Book Out Of You!

horror story. However, she also needed a listening ear because book publishing can be very frustrating. I understood how she felt because I had traveled that road. I let her speak and afterwards I remember hearing a deep breath of relief. We laughed as we continued to converse. At the end of our conversation she was ready to get published. A history making decision and a for sure sign of relief. "Stepping Into A New Place And Time While Letting God Lead You" by Tanisha Burton is a title we all can relate to and many desire. It's a fantastic inspiring book that intrigues the zeal of a mind. This author inspires me for her push. Tanisha Burton refuses to allow anything to hold her new life hostage.

Finally, Tanisha Burton's books arrived on her front porch. All day she had been waiting on the UPS truck. She noticed the truck seemed to have by passed her house. She was startled for a moment because she has been anxious to receive her first shipment of books. Once more she checked her front

It's Time To Get That Book Out Of You!

porch about to question the UPS driver then as she looked down where her books laid. A moment of tears and gratefulness were released. For years she put forth an effort to complete her book. The moment finally arrived, 1/17/2013, a few years later and no journey is worth giving up on especially when it's bigger than you. What a way to bring in the New Year?

Discover the Author in You

For years I did not take "Book Writing Serious" because I did not "MAKE Time to Write," and I did not realize all that was going to come out of me. Your writing is imperative to your destiny. "Make Time to Write!" My writing talents grew from:

1. Book Writing

2. Book Publishing

3. Graphic Art & Design

4. Hosting Seminars & How To Write A Book

5. Marketing You; and

It's Time To Get That Book Out Of You!

6. Transforming News & more... Allow Your Talents to MULTIPLY but the only way is to START with What You Have!

The Authors Choice

The Birth of an Author Shall Be Born *Creative Writing Workshop on How To Write A Book* is for the author in the making. Many do not know how to complete their book or know where to start. I'm deeply inspired by the touching stories after wards. At the end of one workshop this woman came and hugged me. As she was hugging me she also begin to cry and said, **"<u>you do not know how much this workshop has helped me</u>."** Now, I can continue writing! She thought no one would want her book and lost focus on her dream of becoming a published author. Often these are transforming seminars for many whether they use **Fountain of Life Publisher's House or not.** I just love being a part of so many soon to be authors' writing journey. We teach a lot of great tips and highlight dynamic pointers on **How to Write a Book**. Every author in the making needs to attend to

It's Time To Get That Book Out Of You!

sharpen their writing skills! A workshop that will change the way you write forever and help one maintain their focus.

Your Voice Has an Appearance

Your voice matters and it has an appearance through your finished book. Authors are seers of great substance and they will sacrifice to get or obtain what's not visible through the eyesight of others. Your one title can become your household income, your business or a deliverance for others. Through the years, many have come to me to testify about how my books have helped them. I have listed below some great business tips once you finished your book. This is just another way to give your voice an appearance with a paper trail.

Keeping a Money Paper Trail

A few business tips and ways to save for your income tax return. Please always check with your tax preparer because yearly tax breaks and business savings change. However please keep up with all receipts,

It's Time To Get That Book Out Of You!

monthly statements and invoices because it is your paper trail of proof as you are building your business profile. The IRS requires to keep all paper trail on file for at least five consecutive years in case of being audited. Receipts are noted as your outward expense for business operations. So whatever you spend out you will receive a credit on your tax returns and listed below are a few ways you can save. Your new book is a business and if you treat it as one you will be successful. In business be business and you will meet your goal in achieving but you must stick to your plan.

Receipts Are Accountable

Receipts that will cause you to save. Hotel, gas, product, supplies, clothing anything you would spend out to help operate your business is an expense, including dry cleaning. There are so many ways to save. I normally keep yellow envelops and as I enter my office I immediately put my receipts or invoices in. It is also good to record your expense down on

It's Time To Get That Book Out Of You!

paper whether its daily, weekly or monthly but never let one month go by without keeping record. As you review your expense log it will help you maintain a better prospective on your business development.

> Gas
> Hotels & Travel (Business)
> Office supplies
> Dry cleaning
> Cell phone
> Office (Home office expense)
> Insurance
> Vehicle (such as payments and expense for vehicle maintenance)
> Rental car
> Employees (if you are vending or paying someone to help in care of your new book)
> Apparel (pertaining to the upkeep of your uniform appearance)
> Eating out (if you are having a breakfast, lunch or dinner engagement discussing business meeting)
> Health care (doctor visits, doctor bills, medications and yearly insurance payments)

It's Time To Get That Book Out Of You!

- ⟩ Computers, laptops, I Pad, Note Pads, Printers, etc.
- ⟩ Marketing Tools
- ⟩ Advertisements (All ads you place)
- ⟩ Your Stock (Book Orders or any kind of stock)
- ⟩ Shipping & Mailing
- ⟩ Seminar & Conference

Insurance

Also check with your insurance group and prepare to get an author's insurance policy. Yes, there is an insurance policy for the author to protect you and your investment. Some company's offer yearly payments and others will allow you monthly payments. Depending on your liability amount you can get about $100,000.00 policy for about $25.00 a month or $300.00 year and it's worth the investment.

Becoming a Showcase Author

— An author's journey is not easy. There are no guarantees of sales.

It's Time To Get That Book Out Of You!

Authors Corner: Tips for Your New Book

1. Oftentimes new authors do not push their books enough. If you do not Believe in your book it will not sell. Your first book is your branding. You are building a name of recognition when you are a first time author. Here are some key points to help boost your sales as well as Brand Your Name.

2. Book more book signings. Books A Million (BAM) and other book stores will give new authors opportunity but you must Go After It. Call your local book stores and ask to speak to the manger. Ask for opportunity to have a book signing. Have your calendar at hand, your ISBN along with your book title and book a date. Most stores will not have your book on hand so you will have to supply your book signings. Please make sure your books are stocked so that you will not miss an opportunity or sales.

3. Gather your friends, family, neighbors and co-worker to have a book party. You can serve refreshments or have a

cook out. Food will always draw people. The key is to get the word out to the people about your new book. Opportunity is a must when you are branding your name.

4. Make sure your table is set up for conferences, vending and made to attract. Practice on decorating your booth and seek vending opportunities. Invest in your book because your inheritance is in your sales.

5. Invest In Your book appearance while vending. It is a must to attract new readers. Every person that see your table is a potential new reader. It is time you collect.

⟩ Make sure you have a guest registrar at your table to collect potential buyer's information whether they purchase your book or not. That individual is still a potential buyer.

⟩ Candy is always good to lure people to your table.

⟩ Banners are a plus for vending because it advertises you without saying a word. Invest in a banner, post cards, posters, business cards, etc.. Always keep stock on your marketing tools such as postcards, fliers, business cards, website, book marks and more. Any free offers will attract buyers. Some give T-shirts, pens, and cups with their book picture on them. It is a great way to gain more sales.

) Dress to Impress; people are watching you and if your appearance does not fit the description of a successful author, then you will lose sales. People will look at your shoes, clothes, purse, etc., just to see if you have money. Purchase a few new outfits that will also draw good attention. Invest in name brand clothing or fine apparel. It will contribute to boost your sales well as bring recognition to your name. You want good reports all around when you are branding your name. Your outer appearance matters so make it exclusive, professional and fascinating. You can just use those 2-3 outfits for book signings. A professional look will

It's Time To Get That Book Out Of You!

always please your readers. Remember, your name matters. So please care, plan and achieve. You are a successful author and you can greatly succeed.

⟩ Be prepared to discuss your new book or upcoming events with new and potential readers (The one you are working on now.) Authors do not give themselves too much of a break. They always begin a new book to strengthen their writing ability because when you stop the flow stops for writing. The more you write is the more you will flow in writing. It is good to keep your readers excited about your new and upcoming books or events. Let them see you are on the move.

⟩ Talk Shows are always a great outlet. Just find the producer and get their contact information; then seek opportunities to be on their television show. Also be ready to send them your ready marketing materials. Note, the more successful you appear is the better your opportunity will exist.

It's Time To Get That Book Out Of You!

⟩ Don't Quit Trying To Be More Successful

Shaping Your Speaking Introduction

Become the best speaker you can because you can catch or dismiss a sale. Speaking matters and it expresses your personality. Fulfillment comes to those that have a positive attitude, presents good traits of a good character and likeable. Make sure you always show forth a positive spirit to attract new customers. Be ready at all times when you leave your home. Always have your business card in your car or a carrying bag. Practice speaking to people, even in a line, because it increases your ability to speak. Talk to people and make it a good habit to strike up a positive conversation. It is a door opener for you to introduce yourself and present your business card. The more you begin to start new conversations it enhances your speaking ability. Always keep conversation on a professional level. It keeps the door of opportunity open. Practice at home and polish your speaking. Also ask for

It's Time To Get That Book Out Of You!

criticism from a close friend or family member. You can also record yourself through voice or in front of your computer. Once you see yourself you will see what needs to be improved. Also, go to motivational speaking engagements and study different speakers it will help you present yourself better. Remember, practice makes perfect so continue to strive to be the best author you can and to triumph in your visions. I hope for you all the best and never stop trying. The Birth of an Author Shall Be Born. Is it you?

Writing tips for you to be successful

- **Swap extracurricular** time such as relaxation, television, phone conversation, and internet etc., to write. You would be amazed at the PROGRESS You Would Make in SWAPPING TIME. Once you add up one week of extracurricular time you will have gained hours of productive increase to

It's Time To Get That Book Out Of You!

YOUR NEW BOOK. Your page count should be more, your writing ability will be flowing better and the gift of writing should be upgraded. The more progress you make is the closer you will get to the completion of **YOUR NEW BOOK.**

- **Value Your Time** is the best advice I can give you for time is a terrible thing to waste. There is an APPOINTED Time for **YOUR NEW BOOK** to be completed and released. Previously I have put myself on a time schedule to finish a book whether it is a week, month, or days. Putting yourself on a scheduled time to complete YOUR NEW BOOK is always good. It keeps you in remembrance that YOUR NEW BOOK has a schedule to be released.

- **Book Meditation** is medicine to the Author and Zeal for the New Book. A

It's Time To Get That Book Out Of You!

few days out of the week you need to exercise   your thinking ability to increase a writers flow. Your book content needs to give sound instruction, direction and great appeal for you to explain per chapter and segment of your paragraphs. You must keep the interest of your reader in a continuous flow to desire them to want more. So therefore they need to stay entertained, gain awareness or be enticed to want to read further your book. It must flow from book title, chapters and segments to obtain genuine interest for the reader to comprehend your book contents and to refer it to others. Book meditation comes from you allowing your mind to zone into creativity through walking as you think on your new book. Keep in mind what you have written and the next direction on how you want to aim your readers mind in. Your New Book

It's Time To Get That Book Out Of You!

is their entertainment and through your writing you must show them new direction and get them to experience what you see that is the purpose of YOUR NEW BOOK. You can go to a quiet place and get in a meditation zone for your mind to grasp that next directional thought for you to remain on Your New Book journey of expression to your readers. This book meditation will cause you to gain more interest of your new readers to gain the concept of your new book and for them to be fulfilled through your writings. Book meditation is a sure way to help produce a good quality book from a writer's heart.

It's Time To Get That Book Out Of You!

The Birth of An Author

Shall Be BORN

It's a joy being a part of your writing journey and I hope you continue until it's done. Your New Book deserves to live and make sure you obtain the best publishers for your book. We at Fountain of Life Publishers House would love you to come on board. If we can further assist you in book publishing contact us and make sure you get that book out of you. It could be the next New York Times Best Seller or Box Office Hit.

Fountain of Life Publisher's House was founded in 2006 by **Parice C Parker, CEO** and author. Mrs. Parker also experienced the terrible trials of getting published. So, therefore she founded **Fountain of Life Publisher's House,** a place to "House the Voice to Speak in Print." She was gifted with

It's Time To Get That Book Out Of You!

a dynamic vision to help uprising authors to get published and many are finding their way to her. She works hand in hand to ensure the author's publishing journey and to help ease their book publishing process. If Parice C Parker can assist you in anyway possible to publish your book, just call or contact her. **Fountain of Life Publisher's House** is on the rise to obtain every purposed author to be birthed and guided on the right track to their destiny. We offer a wide variety of book publishing services and publishing packages just for you.

It's Time To Get That Book Out Of You!

Phenomenal & Inspiring Books
by Parice C Parker

1) Living Life in A Messed Up Situation
   Volume One
2) Living Life in A Messed Up Situation
   Volume Two
3) Aggravated Assault on Your Mind
4) A Precious Gift from God
5) Word Wonders
6) The Anointing Powers of Your Hands
7) From Eating Crumbs to Transforming
   Wealth
8) The Birth of An Author Shall Be Born

More Soon To Be Released

Visit Our Online Book Store or Where Ever Books Are Sold

www.pariceparker.biz or www.thebookstylist.com

It's Time To Get That Book Out Of You!

Aggravated Assault on Your Mind

Have you ever felt, the very person you have surely loved or believed in has attacked you? It may have been your closest friend, relative, child, your spouse or even yourself. Sometimes you wanted to cry and could not. Shortly afterwards, while gazing about the pain

It's Time To Get That Book Out Of You!

immediately tears began to fall as a flowing river. Your heart has been assaulted and snared with claws of intentions to kill. A multitude of thoughts circulate in your mind and then you began to say to yourself **"How did I let this happen to me?"** Your situation was bound to occur, because somewhere along the way you have allowed your circumstance to control your mind. Allegedly, you put your trust in the wrong one or thing and then you are thrown off guard. Most definitely, you wonder, who do I blame? You did not realize you have entrusted so much of your heart to be assaulted through the passion of love you have given. A since of blindness has overwhelmed your thinking ability, rearranging your life, and throwing it off balance. Truly, there is an explanation and an apology due, but none is ever given. Certainly, you have tried to generate an effectual change. Perhaps, the more you have tried, the more your relationship seemed to die. **Instantly thinking, What Is The Use?**

It's Time To Get That Book Out Of You!

A Precious Gift from God

Your Gift Discovery? It teaches one the value of their natural born talent and motivates one to Live Life On Purpose! This book inspires the heart, gives courage to your *How to Ability* and causes you to live in the pursuit of your happiness. Every natural born leader needs to read this book, it is **AWE – INSPIRING!**

It's Time To Get That Book Out Of You!

Living Life In A Messed Up Situation
Volume One

God will assign the most in-depth spiritual cleaning service through the Blood of Jesus the Christ to clean up your messed up life. **Every messed up situation that you are living** in will have a **Sparkling Effect** when God gets finished with you. Some things He dusts off, others He wipes down and some need to be

It's Time To Get That Book Out Of You!

polished to shine. **Get Polished Perfect** after reading this book and simply gain it all.

It's Time To Get That Book Out Of You!

Living Life In A Messed Up Situation
Volume 2

Living Life In A Messed Up Situation Volume 2: *Astounding ...* It seems though many things has changed within your life including your perseverance. Often you wanted to quit but couldn't afford to even STOP TRYING! As life twirled down so did your hope, dreams and prosperity. Order this book today and Reel In Your Greatest CATCH! A Mega Booster is what you need and this is it! Let JESUS catch You Trying!

It's Time To Get That Book Out Of You!

Word Wonders

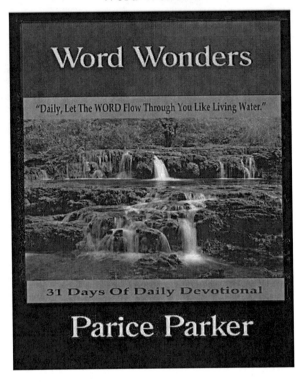

A Eye – Opening ... Word Wonder inspires your HOPE to Greatly Influence your FAITH and it's a magnificent daily devotional book to help keep you focused in word. It EMPOWERS Positive Powers to cause DIVINE FAVOR to ABOUND TOWARDS YOU! Simple things you need to be equipped with more favor from on high. Get This Book TODAY!

It's Time To Get That Book Out Of You!

From Eating Crumbs To Transforming Wealth

Riveting ... Finally, a book that keeps you in a thriving mental state that causes your HOPE to burst through! Now, it is time to identify the real you by introducing the TROPHY that is Hidden inside. It's your time to stop eating the crumbs of life and Indulge In Your WEALTHY Place!

It's Time To Get That Book Out Of You!

The Birth of An Author
Shall Be BORN

If evidence is not your end result then what good is your effort?

~ Parice Parker

It's Time To Get That Book Out Of You!

The Birth of An Author
Author
Shall Be BORN

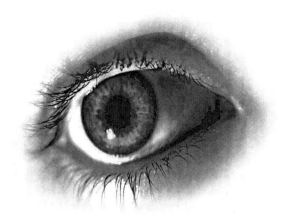

Allow your no to become the fuel of your push.

~Parice Parker

125 *Discover the author in you.*

It's Time To Get That Book Out Of You!

Thank You So Much!

Contact Parice C Parker

www.pariceparker.biz

CPSIA information can be obtained
at www.ICGtesting.com
Printed in the USA
FFOW03n1111070314
.4085FF

9 780991 062713